IN SEARCH OF OWEN ROE

VANESSA O'NEILL

Currency Press, Sydney

CURRENT THEATRE SERIES

First published in 2016
by Currency Press Pty Ltd,
PO Box 2287, Strawberry Hills, NSW, 2012, Australia
enquiries@currency.com.au
www.currency.com.au

in association with La Mama Theatre, Melbourne

Cataloguing-in-publication data for this title is available from the National Library of Australia website: www.nla.gov.au

Typeset by Dean Nottle for Currency Press.
Printed by Fineline Print + Copy Services, St Peters, NSW.
Front and back cover shows Vanessa O'Neill.
Cover photographs by Ponch Hawkes.
Cover design by Katy Wall.

Contents

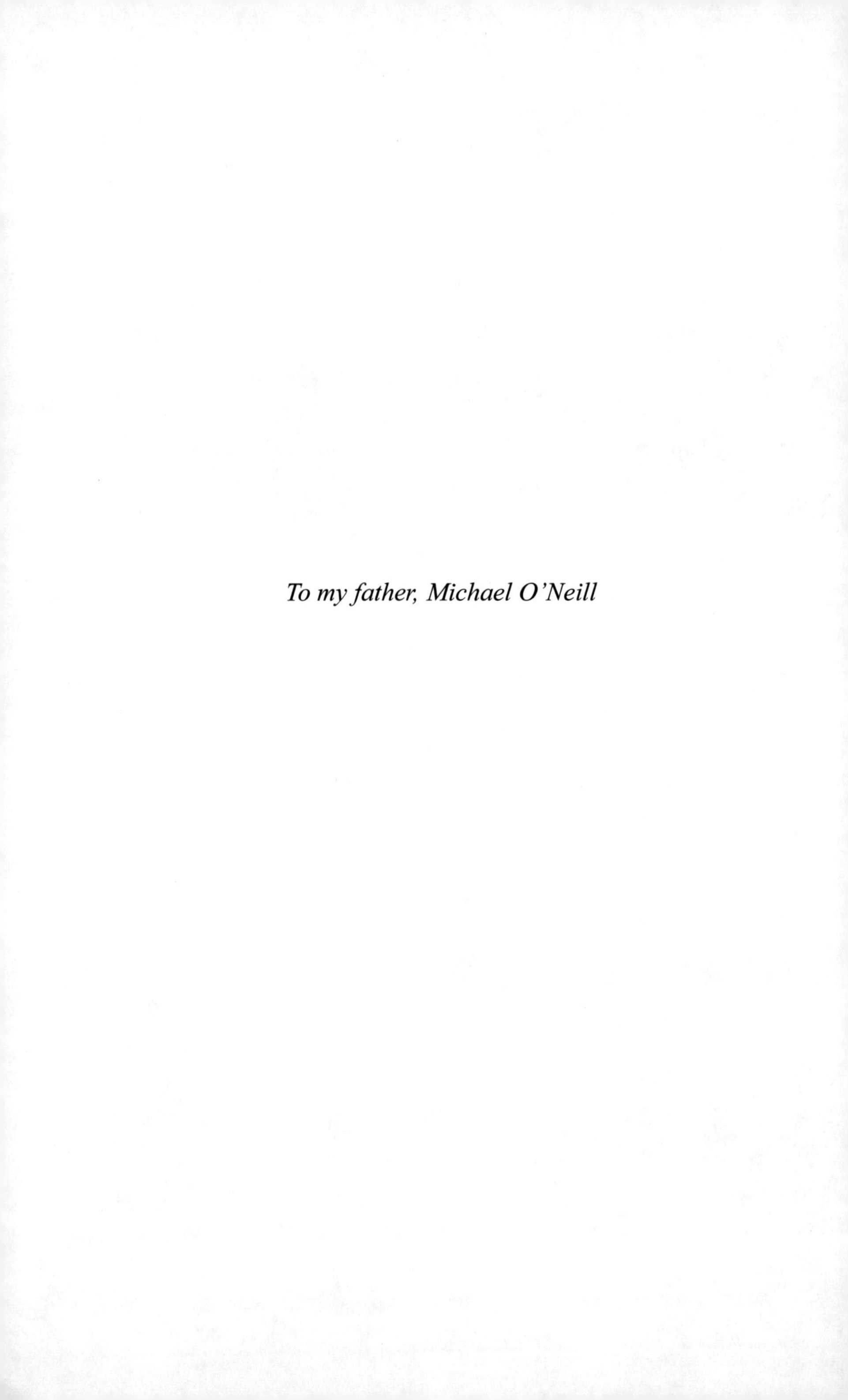

To my father, Michael O'Neill

In Search of Owen Roe was first performed at La Mama Theatre, Melbourne, on 24 June 2015, with the following cast and crew:

Performed by Vanessa O'Neill

Director and Dramaturg, Glynis Angell
Lighting Designer, Richard Vabre
Sound Designer, Darius Kedros
Stage Manager, Sarah McKenzie

Recorded music by the Irish band, Foolin in Doolin

CHARACTERS

NESS, central narrator / storyteller

MARY, Ness's cousin

OWEN ROE ('Red Owen'), leader of the Irish rebellion of 1642

PHILIP O'NEILL, Ness's great-great-grandfather

MIKE O'NEILL, Ness's father

DANIEL O'NEILL, Ness's son

ELLEN MARIA O'NEILL ('Little Grandma'), Owen Roe's second wife and Ness's great-grandmother

AGGIE CHARLOTTE, Owen Roe's first wife

OTHER FAMILY MEMBERS, POLITICAL WRITERS, COURT OFFICIALS, POLICEMEN, SURGEON, WITNESSES, MEDICAL STAFF and JOURNALISTS

All roles are performed by one actor.

The voiceover and soundscape sections feature the voice of the central actor.

SETTING

On the stage left wall is a painted family tree that will have various family members added to it as they are mentioned throughout the show.

Below the family tree is a long coffee table with various memorabilia on it: maps, books, photos, postcards, newspaper clippings, pages from an inquest report, other papers.

On the wall stage right is a large painted map of Ireland, with a small bar table below, and a stool to the side of it.

Further upstage there is a pair of black lace-up boots and a number of empty wine bottles. There is also an old-fashioned apron, a barber's apron hanging on the wall, and a big old chair placed in the upstage corner.

The play is divided into a number of stories. The titles of the stories are not referred to during the production.

PROLOGUE

Pre-show Irish music plays as the audience enters the theatre. The tune, 'Slow Air' (featuring uilleann pipes[1]), is played at key moments during the show.

The lights fade to black.

NESS *comes slowly down the stairs, as if suffering from insomnia, holding a cup of tea. The lighting suggests three or four in the morning. She moves around the space in a dazed state, as if looking for something, wearing a dressing-gown. She then sits on the ground by the table, looking through various papers.*

As she does so, a soundscape starts playing, featuring a whole range of different voices, all of which will feature throughout the play. They include the voices of her father, her son, nursing home staff, Aggie Charlotte, quotes from Macbeth*; all interwoven with sections of Irish music.*

The soundscape builds to a climax. It snaps out with a lighting change to daylight. NESS *discards the dressing-gown and stands centre stage, directly addressing the audience.*

NESS: The O'Neill clan have been summoned. There is to be a gathering.

From the far reaches of various parts of Australia, everyone from the family has been called to Perth. Sisters, brothers, children, partners, grandparents, aunties, uncles, cousins. Ordinarily these people would not all come together. There are too many unspoken grievances, too many past misunderstandings.

There is only one reason that they have come together today. Mikey has called them. And when Mikey O'Neill calls, they answer. Mikey, with the big heart and twinkling eyes, brings out the best in everyone.

The reason for the gathering? The birth of Michael O'Neill's first grandchild. My son: Daniel Michael Kelman O'Neill. The first male grandchild to have the surname O'Neill. And that is worth celebrating.

My father is in his element. Talking and laughing with everybody. Passing around the grandchild for all to admire. Beaming.

---

[1] uilleann pipes are the national bagpipes of Ireland

And as I watch my little boy being passed around—this future O'Neill—I wonder what stories I can tell him about his ancestors. My great grandmother—Little Grandma—is the stuff of legend. Lived until she was one hundred. But what about my great-grandfather who no-one seems to know about? What about Owen Roe O'Neill?

Soundscape of train sounds.

She sways back and forward gently, to signify being on a train.

On a train bound for Cottesloe Beach, later that afternoon. Two hours entirely to myself. I am going to surrender to the depths of the Indian Ocean. I need to wash away the stresses of a morning spent with family members I barely know, trying to explain my bizarre life …

Hot sun on the window, warm train, drifting …

She makes a movement to signify falling into a dream. She speaks as though addressing a circle of relatives—all asking her questions.

Yes, theatre—no, not movies so much, no, not TV—more theatre really—no, not musicals—these little kind of one-woman-shows—storytelling really—no, there's not a lot of money in it … No, Daniel's father doesn't live with us—yes, they do see each other—no, not in our house—yes, it's fine—thanks for asking …

She jolts to signify waking suddenly.

Where am I?

Karrakatta station: the cemetery, where all my relatives are buried. Before I know it I'm off the train …

She wanders through the space, as if looking at an array of grave stones.

I am going to find my great-grandfather's grave. It is meant to be. I'm going to stand and look at his headstone—read the words that were written to remember him by. Bring Daniel back here when he's older …

Such a huge cemetery, so many graves, and my God it is hot. But I know that I will find Owen Roe. I can feel it. My ancestors are calling me. They will lead me to my great-grandfather's grave. Surely …

She stops, noticing a particular grave.

An O'Neill—heaps of O'Neills. There's Grandpa Jack and Grandma Ellen and Auntie Nell and Little Grandma. Where is Owen Roe? He must be close by. Jesus, it is hot …

Call my cousin Mary. She is a lawyer and very sensible. She will know what to do.

MARY: What were you thinking? Didn't you know that the cemetery has a website where you can look up peoples' names? Owen Roe O'Neill. Plot 220. Oh, and he is buried with his daughter.

NESS: Plot 220 …

She searches, then stops at a spot, centre stage.

But there is nothing here. A patch of bare earth.

I had imagined that I would stand at the gravestone of my great-grandfather and cry. Seeing his name written in stone. Linking myself with the Irish heritage that I am so proud of.

How can there be nothing?

Below this bare plot of earth, this unmarked grave, lie the bodies of my great-grandfather, Owen Roe O'Neill, and his thirteen-year-old daughter. A little further away are the graves of all the other O'Neills. Only Owen Roe (and the child buried with him) have nothing. How did my great-grandfather come to be erased from history?

Music fades up.

STORY NUMBER ONE: OWEN ROE O'NEILL (1590–1649)

NESS: You see, you don't just accidently name your eldest son Owen Roe O'Neill. If you give a boy that name, it means something. You are evoking the name of *the* Owen Roe O'Neill—'Red Owen', the famous leader of the Irish Rebellion of 1642.

She places the name 'Owen Roe O'Neill—"Red Owen" 1585–1649' on the wall—beginning the family tree that will be added to throughout the play. She then heads over to the opposite wall—to the map of Ireland.

The music fades out.

Ireland was a pretty wild place in the 1600s—there was no one ruler at the time, but a whole range of clans, kinship groups, lords and chieftains. The O'Neills were part of a powerful and ancient dynasty in Ulster, in the North of Ireland.

The various clans, along with the rugged landscape, made Ireland a difficult country to conquer. And it was a country that completely confounded the English.

In 1609, the Englishman Barnaby Rich in his *Short History of Ireland* wrote that the Irish were …

NESS *takes on the voice and physicality of an upper-class Englishman.*

BARNABY RICH: … more uncivil, more uncleanly, more barbarous and brutish in their customs and demeanours than any other people in the known world.

NESS: Barbarous, brutish, uncivil, unclean savages … my ancestors.

NESS *adds 'Hugh O'Neill—THE GREAT O'NEILL 1540–1616' to the family tree.*

Hugh O'Neill (known as 'The Great O'Neill'—uncle to Owen Roe—and Earl of Tyrone) joined a number of other Irish leaders in fleeing Ireland to seek Spanish help for their battles with the English. This left the North of Ireland vulnerable to attack. It was Owen Roe O'Neill who returned thirty years later to fight these English forces.

I see Owen Roe in my dreams sometimes …

Sounds of bodhrán[2] *drums.*

There is a huge crowd of dark-haired Spaniards—and in amongst them is one tall, red-haired man. He turns to look at me. His blue eyes blazing. There is a fire is his belly, a restlessness, a longing for his homeland. He has been in exile in Spain for so many years now. Serving the Spanish army. Fighting their fights, commanding their troops. And all the while, making appeal after appeal for help to return to Ireland. But now the time has come. His people are calling him.

[*Various Irish voices*] We need you, Owen Roe. Come home now, Owen. Your country bleeds. Heed us!

NESS *walks up and stands on the staircase as if addressing a crowd.*

Sounds from a battlefield gradually build during the speech.

OWEN ROE: I return today to reclaim what is ours. No longer will our people bow to the English. No longer will our customs, our language, and our traditions be outlawed. From today onwards, justice will be done. And as English bones are crushed, and English blood seeps into Irish soil, this green land will once again flourish. Our ancestors will sing, and the shadow that has been cast over us for too long will be lifted. Join with me, my people. Know that we are not alone. Know that our ancestors go with us. They carry and guide us. We shall not fail them! We shall restore their land: our land, and the land of generations to come!

NESS *walks down the stairs to stand by the map of Ireland as the battle sounds fade out.*

NESS: The battle to reclaim Ireland was fought for over seven long years. Ultimately the Irish were defeated. Owen Roe is believed to have been poisoned. And as the man who was recognised as the leader of this rebellion, and the only one believed capable of defeating Oliver Cromwell, his death was initially kept secret, and he was buried in an unmarked grave in Cavan.

---

[2] *bodhrán*, an ancient Celtic drum

Uilleann pipes play.

NESS *speaks in a strong Northern Irish accent:*

Did they dare, did they dare, to slay Owen Roe O'Neill?
Yes, they slew with poison him they feared to meet with steel.
May God wither up their hearts! May their blood cease to flow,
May they walk in living death, who poisoned Owen Roe.

Wail, wail ye for the Mighty One. Wail, wail ye for the Dead,
Quench the hearth, and hold the breath—with ashes strew the head.
How tenderly we loved him. How deeply we deplore!
Holy Saviour! But to think we shall never see him more!

Sagest in the council was he, kindest in the hall,
Sure we never won a battle—'twas Owen won them all.
Had he lived—had he lived—our dear country had been free:
But he's dead, but he's dead, and 'tis slaves we'll ever be.

Wail, wail him through the Island! Weep, weep for our pride!
Would that on the battlefield our gallant chief had died!
Weep the Victor of Beinn Burb—weep him, young and old:
Weep for him, ye women—your beautiful lies cold!

We thought you would not die—we were sure you would not go,
And leave us in our utmost need to Cromwell's cruel blow—
Sheep without a shepherd, when the snow shuts out the sky—
O! Why did you leave us, Owen? Why did you die?

Soft as woman's was your voice, O'Neill! Bright was your eye—
O! Why did you leave us, Owen? Why did you die?
Your troubles are all over, you're at rest with God on high,
But we're slaves, and we're orphans, Owen!—Why did you die? [3]

Music fades up.

[3] From the poem 'Lament for the Death Owen Roe' by Thomas Davis.

STORY NUMBER TWO: PHILIP O'NEILL AND THE BIRTH OF OWEN ROE

The music fades down over the following section of dialogue.

NESS *walks over to the family tree.*

NESS: That 'Lament for the Death of Owen Roe' was written in 1845 by a young Irish nationalist—two hundred years after the death of Owen Roe—Red Owen. The fight for an independent Ireland was still raging.

She adds 'Philip O'Neill 1835–1902' to the family tree.

My great-great grandfather, Philip O'Neill, was living in Ireland at this time—when the lure of gold on the other side of the world took hold of him.

PHILIP O'NEILL: I've heard there's mountains of gold over there. I hear people are fallin' over the stuff. I hear there's sun there too. How hard could it be? It couldn't be any harder than life here—where there's no food and no work. Jaysus—I've got to get on that boat. God knows if I'll survive the journey, but I know I am meant for greater things. I know there's gold in me!

NESS: [*picking up a paper*] I find Philip O'Neill listed in the Melbourne *Argus*, in the Law Reports, charged with insolvency. The causes are …

COURT OFFICIAL: … losses in mining, losses by fire, and being imprisoned for costs of a suit in the County Court. Liability: fifty-six pounds, eighteen shillings; assets: twenty-five pounds; deficiency: thirty-one pounds, eighteen shillings.

NESS: Philip O'Neill appears to have had no success finding gold, but he instead worked as a journeyman hairdresser, around the goldfields and in Bendigo. He married Mary Anne Sheehan of County Tipperary and had seven children. He gave his eldest son a name from his homeland: Owen Roe O'Neill, my great-grandfather.

'Owen Roe O'Neill 1862–1934' is added to the family tree.

NESS *sings in an Irish accent,* bodhrán *drums underneath.*

[*Sung*] Farewell to old Ireland, the land of my childhood,
Which now and forever I'm obliged for to leave.
Farewell to the shores where the shamrock is growing.
It's the bright spot of beauty, the home of the brave.
I will think of her valleys with fond admiration,
Though never again her green hills will I see.
I am bound for to cross o'er the wild swelling ocean
In search of fame, fortune and sweet Liberty.

Lively Irish music plays.

STORY NUMBER THREE: NESS O'NEILL'S LOVE AFFAIR WITH IRELAND

NESS *moves to sit on the stool beside the map of Ireland, listening to the music prior to speaking.*

The music continues to play underneath the following dialogue—fading up and down at various times during the scene.

NESS: Over the last eighteen years I have had seven visits to Ireland. The country gets to me—it gets under my skin, into my heart, my blood, my bones, my soul. Firstly, there is the landscape, that completely takes my breath away, then there is the music that gets to a place deep inside. There are the accents that are sublimely poetic, and finally there are the men, that I have a ridiculous weakness for. So if you were to put me in a pub, in a particularly beautiful part of Ireland, where they happened to be playing traditional Irish music, and seated me beside an Irishman—well, I'd have no chance …

The music swells louder for a few seconds as NESS *stands and smiles towards the chair as though she is a charming Irishman. The music lowers as* NESS *begins.*

CHARMING IRISHMAN 1: Do you mind if we join you? Where are you from? What brings you to Ireland? How long are you staying in Dingle? Can I get you another drink?

NESS: They ask me questions, but I encourage them to speak, and to keep on speaking, on and on. I am at a table with five Irishmen. Heaven! I can barely sit still. My cheeks are still red from the bike ride around the beautiful coast of Dingle, right down in the south of Ireland. Their words are like a balm, cleansing me, whispering to me, lulling me into a state of absolute surrender. I no longer hear words, just sounds, beautiful sounds …

CHARMING IRISHMAN 1: We're going on to another pub, would you like to join us?

NESS: Yes, yes, I would …

A crowded pub in the tiny town of Doolin on the west coast of Ireland. I am watching the singer with the big blue eyes. He smiles at me, and gives me a wink.

CHARMING IRISHMAN 2: Ladies and gentlemen, I have an announcement to make. I have finally found the girl that I am going to marry.

NESS: The pub cheers loudly as he points to me. Then one of the locals says:

SOMEONE IN THE PUB: You be careful with that one now.

CHARMING IRISHMAN 2: Shall we go for a drive?

NESS: Yes, yes, yes!

[*Referring to the map and various parts of Ireland on the wall*] Then there's Philip, the actor who takes me back to his home in Stonybatter, in Dublin, also known as 'Lovey Batter', because so many actors live there. And Martin in Derry, in the North, who takes me home to his parents' house where we sit around the fire and they tell me stories, of life during The Troubles. And the beautiful boy at the youth hostel in Galway who takes me back to stay with his family in lovely Connemara. And Patrick in Glencolumbcille, in the far north-west, who is a photographer, and who introduces me to the wild, rugged beauty of Donegal. There is Haydn, the doctor, with the fancy car and house with a pool in Hollywood, in County Down, who gives me a tour of his house and kisses me in his wine cellar, and Marty the singer who I meet in Belfast, and then again in Dublin. Yes, yes, yes, yes, yes … Because the answer is always yes, when an Irishman is asking the question …

Music fades up.

STORY NUMBER FOUR: MICHAEL O'NEILL AND DANIEL O'NEILL

NESS *moves across the stage to add 'Michael O'Neill 1942–' to the family tree.*

The music fades with the dialogue.

NESS: At the same time as I am engaging in a search for my great-grandfather, my own father—Michael O'Neill—is fading further and further away from me …

MIKE: Ness, you know that I have … you know I have … that, that … oh, oh, what is it?

NESS: Alzheimer's, Dad. Yes, I know.

MIKE: And you know that there is no cure?

NESS: Yes, Dad. But there's is no point in worrying about what is to come.

MIKE: But my memory Ness. It's no good.

NESS: Dad, at least you still know who I am. That's a good thing.

But I do worry. I struggle to see my father for who he is, rather than someone with a disease. Someone with the big 'A' stamped across his forehead. Only my son seems to know how to be completely at ease with his granddad. And my dad is most happy when he is with his grandson.

My son is outside on a tricycle riding round and round in circles whooping. In one hand is a paper kite. In the other is a green plastic golf club that he holds high in the air. Round and round and round. The tricycle is old and faded and way too small for him, found dumped outside someone's house years ago. He has an expensive bike and scooter, but the faded red and yellow tricycle is more fun. Round and round and round. My dad is in the middle, smiling. At ease. Round and round and round. Pure joy, pure pleasure. No agenda and no judgement.

DANIEL: Did you see how good I was? Did you see?

MIKE: Yes, Daniel, I did. You were wonderful.

DANIEL: I did five laps. Now I'm going to do ten laps.

MIKE: Oh, that's terrific, really terrific.

NESS: My father had his licence taken off him. He was driving in an erratic way and a woman called the police and they pulled him over. When I saw him that night he looked like a wounded animal. Someone who was a very long way away. Driving is Dad's freedom: his dignity, his independence. The police instructed Mum to hide his car keys.

POLICEMAN: If he continues to drive he's a danger to everyone.

NESS: My son responds.

DANIEL: Well, he's not a danger to everyone. I mean, he's not a danger to people who live in other countries. Or even in other parts of Australia. So not everyone at all really.

NESS: That evening Dad keeps falling as he walks up the stairs. My mother and I watch helplessly as if in slow motion Dad tries to pour wine into his glass.

She mimes trying to pour wine, with shaking hands.

The red wine circling around the glass onto the tablecloth. My son pats the purple liquid in delight. Dad continues to try to do his usual jobs in the kitchen. Plates in the dishwasher at crazy angles. He moves about the house as if in a trance. Round and round.

I am in Queenscliff at my parents' house. My mother is out shopping.

NESS: Okay, Dad, let's head to the beach …

MIKE: Oh—you go—I'm, I'm … busy here …

NESS: Dad, come on, the kids are in the car. It's beautiful weather. Let's go, Dad …

MIKE: I'm busy … sorting out … with these hoses …

NESS: The hoses can wait, Dad. Let's go …

MIKE: I've got to sort out … I've got work to do … The hoses …

NESS: Dad, come on, the hoses will be here when you get back. The kids want to go to the beach.

MIKE: Then go.

NESS: Dad, we need to take you with us.

MIKE: No … I'm, ah … I've got to … I'm … busy.

NESS: Dad, come on, let's go.

MIKE: No, piss off. I'm busy.

NESS: Oh, for fuck's sake.

DANIEL: Where's Granddad?

NESS: Daniel, can you please get Granddad so that we can go to the beach?

DANIEL: Come on, Granddad. Let's go.

MIKE: Hello little, man. We're going, are we?

NESS: And my dad comes …

[*Directly addressing the audience*] My father is almost always anxious. Except when he is with Daniel, and when I ask him stories about the past.

NESS *gets the chair from upstage and sits in it.*

MIKE: Yes, yes, that's right. Owen Roe O'Neill: the eldest son needed to have that name. I never knew him. He died … before I was … Little Grandma … I'd chop wood for her … I'd ride my bike over and chop wood for her … a little lady, about four foot six. She was fairly dominant. She ran a strict household. That house in Victoria Square … I never knew Owen Roe … My cousin Frankie … he remembered him as a little boy. Said he had beautifully manicured hands. And a bit of a temper. Said Owen Roe threw his dinner against the wall one time … against the wall … The eldest son … he had to be called … Owen … Owen Roe …

Music fades up.

STORY NUMBER FIVE: ELLEN MARIA O'NEILL (1867–1966)

The music fades out with the start of the scene.

NESS *(as* MIKE*) walks—slowing with a small shuffle—in circles, with echoes of her own insomnia.*

NESS *puts on an apron, and takes on the physicality of* LITTLE GRANDMA.

LITTLE GRANDMA: Come on, Mikey, you're a bit late today. Plenty of wood out there for you to chop. Off you go now. Good boy … Come on, Mikey, oh, that's not the end of it. Come on now, Mikey. You listen to your Little Grandma. You don't know how lucky you are. When your father and your aunties and uncles were your age, they were being dragged across the country. Your grandfather got it into his head that the Victorian goldfields were not good enough for him. Oh no, we had to head to the wild west—over to Kalgoorlie. Can you imagine that, Mikey? Me and all the little ones. Then just as we were getting settled we were on the move again. From Kalgoorlie across to Coolgardie, then Boulder, then Fremantle and finally Perth. You're lucky, Mikey, your father is a good, dependable man.

NESS: Little Grandma, as my great-grandmother was known, was twenty-six when she married Owen Roe O'Neill in Bendigo. Owen Roe was thirty-one and a widower when they met.

She adds 'Ellen Maria O'Neill 1866–1966' to the family tree.

Little Grandma's gravestone reads: 'In Loving Memory of our Mother, Ellen Maria O'Neill, 28th October 1966, in her hundredth year'.

Owen Roe was buried in an unmarked grave thirty-two years earlier.

And not one of Owen Roe's children kept the tradition going of naming their eldest son Owen Roe—including Jack, his youngest son and my grandfather.

She adds 'Jack O'Neill 1908–1999' to the family tree as she says his name.

STORY NUMBER SIX: AGGIE CHARLOTTE (1862–1891)

Music comes up.

NESS *removes the apron and transforms into* AGGIE CHARLOTTE *who is swigging from a wine bottle and giggling, and then has moments of shaking, followed by more swigging of wine and laughter. She stands on the chair.*

AGGIE: Happy New Year … Happy 1894!

The music fades and NESS *addresses the audience from centre stage.*

NESS: In my search for Owen Roe, I went looking for his first wife, Aggie Charlotte. The only thing that I'd heard about her was that she had drowned.

She picks up a copy of Aggie's Inquest Report from the table and starts reading from it.

Proceedings of the Inquest held upon the body of Aggie Charlotte O'Neill at The Morgue, Melbourne, January 3rd, 1894.

CONSTABLE DUMBLETON *clears his throat before speaking—standing to the right of the chair.*

CONSTABLE DUMBLETON: Constable A.J. Dumbleton, Burnley Station, Melbourne. I have to report for the information of the coroner that today at five p.m. a man named John V.A. Bruce reported to me that as he was passing down the River Yarra he saw the dead body of a woman floating and snagged to a willow tree. I went to the spot and found a woman as described. I procured a vehicle and conveyed the body to the morgue. She is that of a woman about thirty-five years of age, five foot three inches high, dark hair cut short, stout build, dressed in a reddish-colour dress, white flannel petticoat, with lace trimming around the bottom, white calico chemise, a white calico apron, lace-up boots, no stockings or hat. There are no visible marks of violence on the body. On searching the body I found nothing but a pocket handkerchief. There is nothing suspicious in the case.

JAMES EDWARD NEILD: [*moving to the left of the chair*] James Edward Neild, surgeon, Spring Street, Melbourne. I have made a post-mortem examination of the body of Agnes O'Neill. The stomach contained about a pint and a half of light brown fluid. The contents of the small intestines were of a like character. The cause of death was drowning. The fluid in the stomach seemed to be beer.

MATILDA BARCLAY: [*sitting on the chair*] My name is Matilda Barclay. I am a widow residing at number two Griffin's Lane, off Spring Street in Melbourne. I have seen the body of the deceased and I identify it as that of Agnes O'Neill. She was married, but not living with her husband. She was living in my house. I saw her alive last on Sunday morning between three and four o'clock. She was in the house and was suffering from delirium tremens.

NESS: 'Delirium tremens'—translated from Latin means 'shaking frenzy'—otherwise known as the 'DTs' or 'the horrors', an acute form of delirium brought on by alcoholic withdrawal. Symptoms include insomnia, agitation and hallucinations.

MATILDA BARCLAY: She had been drinking very heavily. She came into the house, laid down for a few minutes, woke up and left the house before I could stop her. She said nothing. I sent down to the watch house. I don't think she had any money on her.

NESS: Matilda Barclay's signature at the bottom of this document is noticeably shaky.

What went wrong? How did Aggie Charlotte end up in the River Yarra on New Year's Eve 1894? What was she even doing in Melbourne? Where was her child? Where was Owen Roe?

She walks over to the family tree, adding 'Aggie Charlotte' to the tree.

This is what I do know: Ten years earlier, Aggie Charlotte McLaughlin, twenty-one, of Kyneton in Victoria, married my great-grandfather Owen Roe O'Neill, also twenty-one, of Clunes in Victoria, at St Paul's Church in Sandhurst. Owen Roe was working as a barber, with his father, Philip O'Neill. They had two children. Maude May, and one unnamed girl, who died at birth.

So what took place over the next decade?

How did Owen Roe respond to the news of Aggie's drowning? How much did he tell his second wife—my Little Grandma—who he married only four months later?

Was he haunted by Aggie Charlotte's death? Is this what drove him to get out of Victoria with his new wife and children—to escape to the wild west, and then to keep on moving?

Round and bloody round …

STORY NUMBER SEVEN: MICHAEL O'NEILL (PART 2)

The music track fades up.

NESS *moves the chair upstage.*

As NESS *paces the floor, the music crossfades to the* VOICEOVER *of a nursing home staff member giving her opinion of* MIKE.

VOICEOVER: I hadn't realised how demented your father was. He is just so bewildered and agitated.

NESS: Demented? You just called my father demented?

VOICEOVER: He is up pacing the corridors every night, going into other people's rooms. He is very confused. He keeps trying to abscond.

NESS: Abscond? Isn't that just a word for trying to get out of somewhere that you don't like? I would have thought that was perfectly rational.

VOICEOVER: He keeps hallucinating, seeing figures in the mirrors. Yesterday he locked two of the carers in a room, he thought they were burglars.

NESS: He thinks he's in his house. He doesn't expect strangers to be in his house. He doesn't want to be in a nursing home. Why would he?

VOICEOVER: I think you are being highly subjective about your father. I am giving you my objective opinion. Your father has advanced dementia. It is for his own good that he is in the dementia ward. He is a risk to himself and others. We just need him to settle.

NESS *shuffles downstage as* MIKE.

NESS: [*to the audience*] When I see my father shuffling along the corridor of the nursing home, he looks like someone has sucked out his soul. But then he sees us, and the light starts to come back into his eyes.

MIKE: Oh, oh … I am so happy to see you, little man, so, so good to see you … Oh this is my grandson, and this is my daughter, oh I have missed you …

NESS: Where are the medical staff now? Where are the nurses, and the doctors, who tell me that my father is demented? Have a look at him.

This man—so full of love—relieved to finally be with people who can see him for who he is.

I can't get my father out of here fast enough. We escape to have lunch by the ocean. Until it is time to take him back there again, back to that dementia ward, tucked away up the back of the nursing home, as though they are the untouchables.

MIKE *is physically trying to resist going back into the nursing home.*

MIKE: [*gesturing to the door*] Let's, let's, let's head back home now. We, we need to get back. Where, where is your mother? Give her a call and tell her that we are on our way, will you? You and Daniel might like to stay the night … Why can't you stay the night? Do you think I'm a leper? Where are we going? Murray Road is back that way … your mother will be expecting us …

STORY NUMBER EIGHT: VANESSA O'NEILL

A soundscape plays of a range of the voices that we have heard in the play so far, as NESS *puts on her dressing-gown and wanders through the space with a cup of tea.*

The lighting is reminiscent of the 'insomnia' lighting at the start of the play.

NESS *takes hold of the range of papers from the table and sits with them on the ground, making a semicircle of papers on the floor, downstage centre.*

The soundscape fades.

NESS: People like to tell me how healthy I am. Recently, a colleague observed:

WORK COLLEAGUE: So, you always seem to drink your own herbal tea? You don't drink coffee or normal tea? And you bring in healthy salads each day for lunch? Don't you have any vices?

NESS: Vices? Don't I have any vices? Let me see now …

Does a ferocious and wild temper count? Does insomnia count? Does thrashing about in the early hours of most mornings in a state of anxiety, self-loathing and panic count? What about the sadness that wakes me at around three or four each morning?

This is my other life, my secret life. As a child I would wake and wander throughout the family house at night in this state. To this day, while the world sleeps, wild thoughts, regrets and raw emotions dance about in my head, taunting and goading me from rest. I stumble out into the morning light, reeling from yet another bout of the craziness that goes on in my head:

MACBETH: [*standing*]

Methought I heard a voice cry, 'Sleep no more!
Macbeth does murder Sleep'—the innocent Sleep;
Sleep, that knits up the ravelled sleeve of care,
The death of each day's life, sore labour's bath,

Balm of hurt minds, great Nature's second course,
Chief nourisher in life's feast …[4]

NESS: I haven't committed a murder—why have I spent so much of my life deprived of sleep? So if I do drink herbal tea and eat salads during the day, it is because I am doing everything I can to counteract the effects of those wild nights. I am doing everything I can to appear sane.

And who the hell was Owen Roe? And why do I even care?

[4] from *Macbeth*, Act 2, scene 2

STORY NUMBER NINE: MY FATHER IS FALLING (RELEASE THE ANGELS)

A soundscape plays. It is a range of sounds from the nursing home—daytime television, cheesy songs, beeps, alarms, PA announcements, and a woman who repeatedly cries out—'Help me, help me, please help me'.

Then the VOICEOVER *of a nursing home staff member begins to play over the continuing soundscape as* NESS *shuffles slowly across the stage as* MIKE.

VOICEOVER: Your poor father. I feel so sorry for him. It is such a shame, such a terrible shame. He is a danger to himself. We simply cannot watch over him all the time. We have twenty-three other residents to attend to. We are going to need to restrain him. It is for his own good. It is in his best interests. You do understand that, don't you?

During the VOICEOVER, *a sequence takes place where* NESS *(as Mike) tentatively tries to climb the stairs but keeps stumbling, finally falling all the way down to the door at the end of the stairs.*

NESS: My father is falling.

His body has been letting him down. The will is still there. The determination and stubbornness are still there.

She starts to walk tentatively as her father.

That he can walk. That he can move. That he is free. And his first few steps are taken with great confidence. I try to help him, to hold him steady. He pushes me away. Enjoys his freedom. Stepping. Unassisted. And then with no warning at all …

She falls to the ground.

My son and I watch helplessly. Pain and shame in his eyes.

What is it with falling? We fall asleep. We fall in love. We fall in and out of consciousness. Falling into other realms, altered realities, alternative states of being. And then there is falling through walls, crashing over television sets, into doors and onto bathroom floors.

She stands.

My father is covered in bruises and cuts—all testaments to the fight that lives on within him. Of his need to exert his own free will. But his body keeps on betraying him.

And then they harness my father to a chair.

She uses the tie on her dressing-gown to tie herself to the railing at the bottom of the staircase. As she speaks the following text she tries to break free.

Strap him in. He pulls at the harness. Confused to have yet another restraint placed upon him. Is it not enough that they have locked him up in this place, or that they fill his body with an assortment of drugs every day? Now they need to tie him down as well. I try to take him outside in a wheelchair. And he does all he can to obstruct this form of travel. Reaches down to put on the brakes. Places his feet on the ground so that we cannot move. Holds onto doorways and poles, to let me know that there is a spirit stirring within him. He may have lost his ability to speak, to walk, to toilet, shower, feed and dress himself. But he has not been tamed. And he has not surrendered.

She releases herself from the harness and takes off the dressing-gown.

Every part of me cries out that no good can come of my father being in this place. It is hastening his decline at a ridiculous rate. But I can say nothing. I have been told not to be difficult. I have been told not to be a troublemaker. I have been told to accept that there is nothing that can be done. What's done cannot be undone …

LADY MACBETH: Ohhhh … Wash your hands; put on your nightgown, look not so pale—I tell you yet again … he cannot come out on his grave … To bed, to bed: there's knocking at the gate. Come, come, come, come, give me your hand. What's done cannot be undone. To bed, to bed, to bed …[5]

A soundscape starts to build very slowly, commencing with bodhrán *drums.*

[5] from *Macbeth*, Act 5, scene 1

NESS: But I cannot sleep because there are voices that will out, that will not be silenced. They urge me to make trouble. I want to be a troublemaker. I come from a long line of troublemakers. When Owen Roe—Red Owen—returned to Ireland, it was to make trouble, to set alight the fires of resistance amongst his people …

NESS *runs up the staircase and speaks out to the audience.*

OWEN ROE: Throw those arrows, go on, burn those bridges. The fire that seethes within you, set it free! Go on—I dare you! Set the world ablaze. Do it! Go on! You know you want to …

NESS: I want to release those dear souls in the dementia ward. Those beautiful beings, who have been hidden away in that locked, cramped space. Fly, my beauties, fly—triumphantly through the air. And my dear father—rise up—I give you back your dignity. I give you back your light and your fire. I give you back your freedom. Rise up and fly—you who are descended from the great O'Neills—from mighty kings and warriors.

She runs down the stairs into the auditorium and opens the doors on either side of the theatre. Light floods in from each door.

Abscond, abscond, to your heart's content—arise, all of you, like angels. And to those of you who could not see their beauty, stay behind in that locked and stinking ward.

She stands centre stage looking up in the air.

And stare up in amazement at these beautiful free beings, as they fly away, laughing wickedly as they go.

The soundscape of laughter, drums, battle sounds and music builds to a climax and then fades out.

NESS *walks in silence to close the doors and pick up all of the papers on the floor.*

STORY NUMBER TEN: OWEN ROE O'NEILL (1862–1934)

NESS: Owen Roe is eluding me. I know a few facts about his life—but I still haven't been able to work out who he really was. Of all my ancestors, he's the one who is most interesting to me. I've been desperate to find out whether there is something different about him, something transgressive. I am searching for a fellow black sheep amongst my ancestors.

She continues sifting through papers.

So I keep on looking and looking and looking. And then I strike gold.

She reads from a newspaper article:

Thursday, third of May 1934. *Daily News*, Perth. Headline: 'STATE'S OLDEST BARBER DIES'.

VOICEOVER: [*a 1930s newsreader*] Believed to be the oldest barber in the state, Mr Owen Roe ('Garry') O'Neill died on Tuesday. The funeral took place yesterday at Karrakatta. Born in Victoria, the late Mr O'Neill came to this state about forty-five years ago, and followed his trade as a barber in various hairdressing establishments in Perth. Highly popular with his customers, he had a large number of friends. Many prominent members of the community can recall the times when 'Garry', as he was called, attended to their needs when they were youngsters. Aged seventy-two years, the late Mr O'Neill left three daughters and three sons.

NESS: Garry? Garry? I've taken this long to find out who my great-grandfather was, and when I finally do, I discover that rather than use the name he was given of the famous Irishman, Owen Roe O'Neill, he was known as Garry! What's that about?

She takes out another piece of paper and reads from it.

And then I find another article. Wednesday, ninth of May 1934. *Daily News*, Perth:

As the next VOICEOVER *plays,* NESS *places the various papers back on the table and moves the upstage chair to centre stage, puts on the barber's apron and takes out an old-fashioned razor from the pocket. She wipes it on the side of the apron, and goes through a series of stylised movements of a barber in action.*

VOICEOVER: [*another 1930s newsreader*] From 'A Window in Perth: The Chair is Vacant': One wonders how often in his long experience in haircutting and shaving the late Owen Roe O'Neill said, 'Next please'. From his early days when he helped in his father's saloon in Pall Mall, Bendigo, until his retirement not so long ago, he had a wealth of experiences at his trade and the procession of 'Next pleases' in Bendigo, Fremantle, Coolgardie, Boulder, Kalgoorlie, and Perth must have seemed interminable. Seventy-two and a half years of age at the time of his death in Victoria Square, Perth, he had had thirty-seven years of busy life in this state, and was recognised as the doyen of the profession.

He devoted some of his time to wig making, and found much employment for his skill in the branch of the trade, first among the amateur theatricals of Bendigo and later on the goldfields and in Perth. This side of life gave him many stories of experiences with footlight personalities, and he was an interesting raconteur who could while away a spare half-hour for people who liked to dig into earlier days' history. Popular with a legion of patrons, many of whom have preceded him on the Westward journey, he is gratefully remembered for his engaging temperament, and his widow, three sons and two daughters who survive him have received many evidences of sympathy in their bereavement.

NESS: All this for a man who will end his days beneath a bare plot of earth …

She puts the barber's razor back in the apron pocket.

I manage to get hold of my dad's cousin Frankie, the only living person who has a memory of Owen Roe, albeit as a very young boy. He tells me that despite the fact that Owen Roe worked as a barber from a very young age right up until he died—quite a bit of his money went on drink. So when their eldest daughter died, she was buried in an unmarked grave, as that was all the family could afford at the time.

VOICEOVER: [*an old-fashioned-sounding recording*] O'Neill—Zilliah Goldsmith (Queenie) O'Neill, eldest daughter of Owen Roe (Garry) O'Neill, aged thirteen years and seven months.

NESS *speaks the following sentence with the* VOICEOVER*; the* VOICEOVER *fades out by the end of the sentence:*

VOICEOVER & NESS: [*together*] Bendigo and goldfields papers, please copy.

NESS *kneels centre stage, as if looking at the plot of land where Owen Roe and Zilliah are buried.*

NESS: A tired angel fallen late into a gentle slumber. Rest in peace.

And it is her unmarked grave that Owen Roe will be buried in twenty-six years later.

Music up as NESS *removes the apron and places it on the back of the barber's chair.*

Owen Roe O'Neill. An interesting raconteur, a storyteller who liked to dig into earlier days' history, and had experiences with footlights personalities. A man whose work as a men's hairdresser took him from one side of Australia to the other. A weaver of words. A bon vivant and a drinker. My great-grandfather was ultimately remembered for his ability to tell interesting stories.

Owen Roe wasn't erased from history at all. He didn't get a headstone, but he was publicly celebrated.

I'd love to know what stories he told—but I'd also love to know the stories that remained secret.

This is a story that began with nothing. A need to know what lay beneath a bare patch of earth. What I found was a fellow storyteller, a fellow wanderer, and in all likelihood a fellow troublemaker.

Rest in peace, Owen Roe—Garry …

She goes back up the stairs as the music fades out.

THE END

presents

IN SEARCH OF OWEN ROE

11–28 May 2016

Writer
Vanessa O'Neill

Director and Dramaturg
Glynis Angell

Set Designer
Annie Edney

Sound Designer
Darius Kedros

Lighting Designer
Richard Vabre

Stage Manager
Sarah McKenzie

Music Composition
**Foolin in Doolin: Karol Lynch,
Michael O'Connell, Cyril O'Donohue**

Production Photography
Sarah Walker

Performed by **Vanessa O'Neill**

CEO & Artistic Director
Liz Jones

Company Manager and Creative Producer
Caitlin Dullard

Communications
Nedd Jones

Technical Manager
Bec Etchell

Front-of-House Manager
Amber Hart

Development Coordinator
Mary Helen Sassman

Office Administrator
Elena Larkin

Media & Creative Communications
Stefania Di Gennaro

La Mama Learning Producer
Maureen Hartley

Preservation Coordinator
Fiona Wiseman

La Mama for Kids Curator
Ella Holmes

La Mama Musica Curator
Annabel Warmington

La Mama Poetica Curator
Amanda Anastasi

Script Appraiser
Graham Downey

Groundsman
Chris Molyneux

Interns
Zac Kazepis, Caitlin Zacharias, Roisin Lynagh

Level 1, 205 Faraday Street, Carlton VIC 3053
www.lamama.com.au | info@lamama.com.au
facebook.com/lamama.theatre | twitter.com/lamamatheatre
Office phone 03 9347 6948 | Office hours Mon–Fri, 10:30am–5:30pm

Our sincerest thanks to the many volunteers who generously give their time in support of La Mama.

La Mama's Committee of Management, staff and its wider theatrical community acknowledge that our theatre is on traditional Wurundjeri land.

The La Mama community acknowledges the considerable support it has received in the past decade from Jeanne Pratt and The Pratt Foundation.

La Mama is financially assisted by the Australian Government through the Australia Council – its arts funding and advisory body, the Victorian Government through Creative Victoria – Department of Premier and Cabinet, and the City of Melbourne through the Arts and Culture triennial funding program.

PLAYWRIGHT-PERFORMER'S NOTE

Ten years ago I was in Perth for a large family gathering, organised by my father, to celebrate the birth of his first grandchild: my son, Daniel. I made a spur-of-the-moment decision to go to Karrakatta Cemetery, to visit my great-grandfather's grave. The discovery that Owen Roe O'Neill was buried in an unmarked grave, alongside one of his daughters, stayed with me long after I returned home to Melbourne.

Five years later, I was offered a place on the Victoria University Solo Residency. This gave me the opportunity to spend a year developing a solo piece of theatre. In the first meeting with my mentor, Ben Rogan, I spoke about the mystery of my great-grandfather, which no living family member could explain to me. I had a feeling that there were stories to be uncovered. The fact that he was named after a famous Irish rebellion leader from the 1600's, and linked me back to Ireland, only added to his appeal.

I uncovered a number of stories about my great-grandfather, as well as other family members. I went back to Ireland for my seventh visit, and rekindled my love of that country. I found newspaper articles, inquest reports, music, ballads, poems, photos and other historical documents: all of which provided the raw material for this work.

The following year, I travelled to the UK to be part of the International Actors' Fellowship at Shakespeare's Globe. I spent four weeks training and performing with actors from around the world. During this time I was taught by the formidable Glynn MacDonald (known as 'Mother Globe') about the origin of the word 'sincere' – which, according to her, is the Latin for 'without wax'. Glynn explained that this related to religious statues that usually had their cracks and flaws covered with wax. Those that had their flaws uncovered, were 'sincere' – pronounced 'sincheeray'. Glynn explained that on the Globe stage, there was nowhere to hide. We had to apply a 'sincere' approach to our work on that stage.

Back in Australia, I started work with director/dramaturg Glynis Angell. We decided to apply the concept of 'sincheeray'/'without wax' to *In Search of Owen Roe*. Our aim has always been to tell the stories with honesty, boldness and sincerity. La Mama's *Explorations* season gave us the opportunity to test the work over three nights. The sixty-five pages of audience feedback that we received informed further development, up to the play's first full season last year.

This is a play that began with nothing. A bare plot of earth, and a subsequent search for the great-grandfather buried beneath. The stories woven throughout the piece have taken on lives of their own, leading to unexpected areas, with surprising echoes across different characters and sources. At the heart of the play is the story of my own father, Michael O'Neill, whose memory began to fade just as I was uncovering information about his grandfather, Owen Roe O'Neill.

It is a great pleasure to revisit this work for a return season at La Mama Theatre and a subsequent tour with Regional Arts Victoria. I am indebted to my wonderful team: Richard Vabre for his superb lighting design, Darius Kedros for his extraordinary sound design, Annie Edney for her beautiful set pieces, Sarah McKenzie my fearless stage manager, and Glynis Angell, for guiding me with such grace through the rehearsal and script development process. Special thanks to Foolin in Doolin for permission to use their beautiful music throughout the show.

I am grateful to Greg Dyson and Victoria University for providing artists with the space to freely explore new solo work. And to Ben Rogan, the wise and patient mentor, who encouraged my first tentative steps with this work. And finally a big thank-you to La Mama Theatre for their ongoing support of new Australian work. It is an honour to perform this play in their magical theatre.

Vanessa O'Neill

Writer and performer

PRODUCTION NOTES

SET

Annie Edney created two key set pieces to hang either side of the La Mama Theatre stage. Both feature Celtic designs and a rich golden colour, to suggest age and to add warmth to the space. They were designed to be very easy to tour with. On the audience's right is a Celtic family tree that has the names of the O'Neills added to it over the course of the play. It is designed to help the audience keep track of the various family members. On the audience's left is a map of Ireland, featuring the names of some of the places referred to during the play. Ireland is central to this production—a place of deep significance for many of the characters in the play.

PROPS

The most significant props are the source materials referenced in the play: newspaper articles, inquest reports, birth certificates, historical books, photographs, travel books and a copy of *Macbeth*.

SOUND

Darius Kedros has mixed together a number of tracks from the Irish band, Foolin in Doolin, with a soundscape that features characters and text from throughout the play. This enhances the feeling of memories swirling around the stage—at times haunting the central character, at other times echoing between different characters and time periods. Other mixed elements include Irish *Uillean* pipes and *Bodrain* drums, and the sounds of the battlefields and the nursing home.

LIGHTING

Richard Vabre's lighting design helps enhance mood and gives a sense of place within the intimate, minimal theatre set. His use of colours in particular helps transform the space, to enhance the changes between characters, times, and places.

THE O'NEILLS
KEY NAMES AND DATES

- OWEN ROE ('RED OWEN'), 1585–1649: Leader of the Irish Rebellion of 1642
- HUGH O'NEILL ('THE GREAT O'NEILL'), 1540–1616: Earl of Tyrone
- PHILIP O'NEILL, 1835–1902: Great-great-grandfather of Ness O'Neill
- OWEN ROE O'NEILL, 1862–1934: Great-grandfather of Ness O'Neill
- AGGIE CHARLOTTE O'NEILL, 1862–1891: Owen Roe's first wife
- ELLEN MARIA O'NEILL ('LITTLE GRANDMA'), 1866–1966: Great-grandmother of Ness O'Neill and Owen Roe's second wife
- JACK O'NEILL, 1908–1999: Grandfather of Ness O'Neill
- MICHAEL O'NEILL, 1942–: Father of Ness O'Neill
- DANIEL O'NEILL, 2005–: Son of Ness O'Neill
- VANESSA 'NESS' O'NEILL: Central narrator / storyteller

VANESSA O'NEILL
PLAYWRIGHT, PERFORMER

Vanessa O'Neill trained as an actor at the Ecole Philippe Gaulier and at the Drama Centre in London. She has worked for a range of theatre companies including The Australian Shakespeare Company, La Mama, Shakespeare by The Sea, Harlos Theatre Company, Sydney Art Theatre, Bell Shakespeare, and The Arts Centre, Victoria. From 2001 to 2004 she toured her one-woman show *Happy With Half Your Life* across Australia, the UK and Europe, with the assistance of The Australia Council for the Arts. Vanessa has toured schools throughout Australia with a solo show of *Shakespeare's Women*. In 2013, Vanessa took part in the International Fellowship at Shakespeare's Globe. She is currently the Youth and Education Manager at Malthouse Theatre.

GLYNIS ANGELL
DIRECTOR, DRAMATURG

Glynis Angell is a theatre maker, actor, director and teacher. Her directing and dramaturgical work includes projects with performing artists: Ilan Abrahams *Drago's Amazing Bona Fide Freak Show*, Kate Hunter and Emillie Collyer *Maybe We're Never Together* (Big West Festival), Kate Hunter *list(n)*, and Penny Baron *The Lab*. Glynis has devised works with companies including The Business and Hunchback Theatre. Glynis co-wrote and performed the show *Haul Away,* which was nominated for Best New Australian Play Green Room Awards 2006.

ANNIE EDNEY
SET DESIGNER

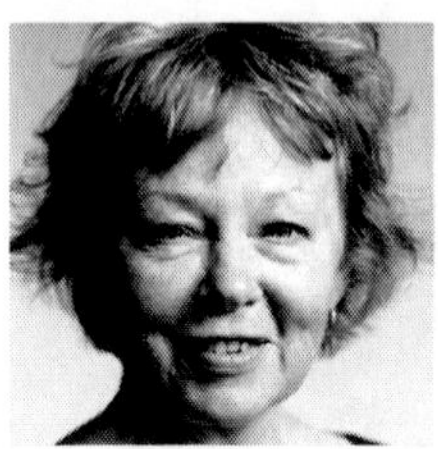

Annie Edney is a multi-disciplinary Melbourne-based artist whose work offers excerpts from heart, memory, dreams and academic research. In her studio practice, Edney is currently exploring a new visual language for our human relationship with the planet, via semi-abstract tondo-focused video and photography. Edney has extensive experience creating site-specific celebratory events with themes of environment and social harmony. She is represented in private and public collections including the Museum of the Riverina, Macquarie University, and the Abbotsford Convent.

DARIUS KEDROS
SOUND DESIGNER

Sound artist, sound designer, composer and music producer **Darius Kedros** works across art installation, radio & performance. Since relocating to Melbourne from the UK in 2013 he has created work for the ABC's Radio National, the Festival of Live Art, Scienceworks, Federation Square, Fortyfive Downstairs, Barking Spider Visual Theatre, Big West Festival & the State Library of Victoria. Australian artist collaborations include projects with Susie Dee, Triage Live Art Collective, Matt Scholten, Kathy Holowko, Lina Limosani & Tim Minchin. His northern hemisphere collaborations & credits include The Rambert Dance Company, Momentum Pictures, BBC, V2 & Virgin Records, Nellee Hooper, Kathryn Williams, Jon Spencer and Craig Armstrong.

RICHARD VABRE
LIGHTING DESIGNER

Richard Vabre is a freelance lighting designer who has lit productions for MTC, STC, Malthouse Theatre, Belvoir Street, Victorian Opera, Windmill Theatre, Arena Theatre Company, NICA, The Darwin Festival, Stuck Pig's Squealing, Chambermade, Rawcus, Red Stitch, Polyglot, Melbourne Worker's Theatre, Aphids and many, many productions at La Mama. Richard has won four Green Room Awards including the Association's John Truscott Prize for Excellence in Design (2004). He has been nominated for an additional seven Green Room Awards.

SARAH MCKENZIE
STAGE MANAGER

Sarah McKenzie is a freelance stage manager and production manager who studied Live Production and Technical Theatre at Melbourne Polytechnic. She has worked for The Rabble, Red Stich, Antony Hamilton Projects, Stone/Castro, Here Theatre, Polyglot, Rawcus, Platform Youth Theater, Gasworks and La Mama. Credits include *Coranderrk: We will show the country,* (part of the ongoing *Minutes of Evidence* project), *Little Black Bastard* (Noel Tovey) and *Nyx* (Melbourne Festival).

STANDING OVATION FOR AUSTRALIA'S HOME OF INDEPENDENT THEATRE

In 2016, La Mama will celebrate 49 years of nurturing new Australian theatre.

Built in 1883 for Anthony Reuben Ford, a Carlton printer, the building at 205 Faraday Street had been used as a workshop, a boot and shoe factory, an electrical engineering workshop and a silk underwear factory before becoming a theatre in 1967. La Mama was established by Betty Burstall and modelled on experimental theatre activities at La MaMa E.T.C., New York. Jack Hibberd's play *Three Old Friends* was the first play performed in the tiny space.

Since that time the crowded intimacy of La Mama has provided welcome opportunities to a host of playwrights, actors, directors, technicians, film-makers, poets and comedians, such as David Williamson, Barry Dickins, John Romeril, Tes Lyssiotis, Lloyd Jones, Arthur and Corinne Cantrill, Judith Lucy, Richard Frankland, Julia Zemiro, and Cate Blanchett ... the list of those who have been nurtured there is long.

Under the capable care of Liz Jones (Artistic Director since 1976), and her La Mama team, more than 50 productions are now produced annually at La Mama, and at our second performance venue, the refurbished La Mama Courthouse, 349 Drummond Street. An ever-increasing audience is drawn not only from the Carlton and Melbourne University environs, but from far and wide across the country.

'I set La Mama up, as a space for writers and directors to perform in but also it was a space where people came, as audience, to participate in the creative experiment.'

—Betty Burstall, Artistic Director of La Mama 1967–76

'Much will be said of La Mama's role in developing a new generation of Australian writing. However, in considering policies and personalities, one should not forget the nature of the space and its impact in making possible performances that would be lost in a large theatre. It gave performances the intimacy of the cinema close-up with the exciting immediacy of the live theatre and the warmth of the coffee lounge.'

—Daryl Wilkinson, Director

La Mama Theatre—which, on various occasions, has been called headquarters, the source, the shopfront and the birthplace of Australian theatre—was classified by the National Trust in 1999.

'The two story brick building is of State cultural significance because it has been occupied by La Mama Theatre... The building is indelibly associated with the performance arts and is a rare manifestation of an experimental theatre in Australia...'

—National Trust Classification Report

When it comes to grassroots Melbourne theatre, La Mama in Carlton is like the 60GB iPod—small, subtle, but containing a whole lot more than you might expect.

—John Bailey, *Age*

La Mama produces work from two venues: 205 Faraday Street, Carlton (opposite top), and at the La Mama Courthouse, 349 Drummond Street, Carlton.

For current La Mama productions and events, see www.lamama.com.au.